地球国創世
（キリストは黒人）

The Earth Nation Creation
（Jesus Is A Brother）

JN035223

The Earth Nation Creation
Jesus Is A Brother

by Auntie Yaka

目次

Index

はじめに

　まず最初に、サブタイトル Jesus Is A Brother について、なぜこのようなこと事を今さら言うのか？
　知っている人は知っている事なのに…？
　その理由を申し上げます。

1, ひとりでも多くの世の中の人々に真実を知ってもらいたい。
2, なぜなら、神は『Judgement day の時、私を知らない者は私もあなたを知らない』と言っているからです。
＊Judgment day とは、最後の審判・神の裁き

　せっかく神様の存在を知り理解していても頭の中に違うイメージ（容姿）で認識していたら、

　Judgement day の時、神様に会わせてもらうために まず Jesus に会うか（Jesus は神様とつながるためのパスポート）神様の傍らに Jesus がいる（神様とキリストは 1つ）訳ですが、
　今現在ほとんどの皆さんは Jesus（キリスト）は 青い目でブロンドヘアーの白人だと思い込んでいるのでは？
　しかし本当は、Jesus は黒人（Brother）です。
　なぜ黒人（Brother）か？

1, その時代（今から約 2000 年前）その土地（現在のイスラエル地方）の人々は有色人種である。

Prologue

First of all, why do I say such a thing now, about the title of this book "Jesus Is A Brother."

There are many people who already know the truth of Jesus. Well I`ll tell you why.

1, I want the world to know the truth, as many people as possible.

2, Jesus said [If you do not know me in the day of judgment, I will know you not]

*The final judgement given by Jesus after death.

Even if you know and understand the existence of God, but accept false images of the Lord that are not true.

On Judgement day, Jesus will appear and you will be afraid of him. (Jesus is the passport that connects with God) or Jesus will be beside God, but they are one.

Perhaps right now, I think most people believe that Jesus (Christ) is a Caucasian with blond hair and blue eyes.

Actually Jesus was a person of color(Brother).

Why is it so?

1, During that period (about 2000 years ago) people of that region were of color.

2，Bible（聖書）に Jesus の容姿について髪は羊の毛（ク
リクリの巻き毛）のようで、肌の色は地球の色、すなわ
ち土色、旧日本式に言うと土人＝黒人と言う訳です。

　では、なぜ Jesus は白人に替えられてしまったのでし
ょうか？
　その答えは簡単です。
　昔から人間は権力、支配力を欲しがりました。

　今でも地球上の一部の人々はその欲にかられています。
昔から白人は戦略、略奪をくり返し、北米、南米、オー
ストラリア、アフリカ諸国、アジア諸国、イスラエル等
世界中を自分達の国と言って横取りして来ました。

　日本人も最近まで近隣アジアの国々に同じような事を
して来ました。

　今、人はもうここへ来て過去の過ちをまず認め、悔い
改め、そして正す必要があるのでは？
　人道的と言うより神の教えから（Righteousness）正し
い事は正しい、間違っている事は間違っていると。

2, The bible says, the hair of Christ is curly(nappy/kinky) like lambs wools, his skin tone is like that of the earth.
(old Japanese way to say DOJIN equal black man)

Then why has Jesus been changed to caucasian?

The answer is simple.
The human being wanted power, dominance from long ago.

Some people on the earth are still seized with that desire. Most caucasians repeated a strategy plunder from old days.
The caucasians plunder North America, South America, Australia, African countries, Asian countries, and Israel by force. Then they called it their own country. They seized the land from native people.
The Japanese did similar things in neighboring countries of Asia too.

We've come so far, but there is a need to acknowledge past mistakes, repent and correct them by God's rule (Righteousness) Right is right, wrong is wrong, rather than man made rule,

1、地球国に必要な5つのキーワード

　現在 地球上ではたくさんの人々が平和を願って生きています。

　しかし、同じく現在地球上では たくさんの戦争や飢餓や貧困や病気で多くの命が失われています。現在地球上で起きているほとんどの不幸や 苦悩は無くせます。

　その答えはとても簡単です。
　地球上の国々がひとつの国、地球国になるのです。

　そんな事が可能か？と思う人がいるかも知れませんが考えてみて下さい。ほんの少し前まで今現在は ひとつの国もいくつもの国に分かれていました。

　たとえば日本も西と東とに分かれて関ヶ原の戦いをしたり、アメリカも北と南とに分かれて南北戦争をしていましたが今は両国とも一国です。

　当時は乗り物も馬の時代で人々の視野も行動範囲も狭かった訳ですが、今日それはズームアップされ地球規模で見る時代です。
　スペースシャトルに乗った宇宙飛行士の目から観た地球は、素晴らしい青い惑星で国境線など見えないのです。なぜなら、元々そんなもの無いのですから。国境線はどん欲で愚かな人間が勝手に作ったものです。

1、 *Five keywords that the Earth Nation need*

Now many people are striving for "hope of peace" on earth.

But also, at the same time many lives are lost by wars, starvation, poverty and diseases. To eliminate most of the misery and suffering that is happening on earth today,

The answer is very easy.

Countries on the earth become one nation! The Earth Nation.

You might wonder is this possible? Please just think back one country was divided into many countries, it wasn't so long ago.

For example, Japan parted the west and the east, causing the Battle of Sekigahara. The United States was divided into north and south, causing the Civil War, but now both countries are one.

Back then transportation was mainly by horse, also people's vision and range of action was small. But now we zoom up and see and move on a global scale.

From the astronaut's eyes on the space shuttle, the earth is a wonderful blue planet, and there is no borderlines. Because originally there was not such a thing. Foolish human beings made the borderlines by acts of greed without permission.

地球上で平和に暮らす動物達（クジラや渡り鳥）の目にも国境線など無いのです。地球上に暮らす多くの人々がこの意見に共感・賛同してくれて それに向かって動き出せば現実になる日もそう遠くはないでしょう。地球国の良い点はたくさんあります。

1、　今現在どの国も膨大な金額を費やしている『軍事費・防衛費』ですが これを使って多くの問題を解決する事が出来ます。一国になれば敵がいなくなるのですから戦う必要が無くなる。

　たとえば、自分の右腕 が自分の左足を傷つけよう やっつけようなどと思う訳がないし、もしそうしたらそれは結局自分自身の体なのだから自分が苦しむ。もう１つ言えば現在の福島県が岡山県を攻撃するなどという事はRidiculous（バカげている）。

　では、その各国の膨大な防衛費を何に使うか？

　地球国を防衛するために使うのです、何から？

　そう、それは 森林破壊、干ばつ、オゾン層破壊、地球温暖化、天災（台風・地震・ 津波・環境破壊〈これは人災？〉）などから守るために使うのです。熱帯雨林を作るのです。

Like most animals living peacefully on earth (whales and migratory birds) do not have borderlines. If people on earth world agree with this opinion, and start moving towards human harmony it wouldn't be long before unity becomes a reality. There are many good points about the Earth Nation.

1, Many countries spend huge "amounts of money on military defense". Leaders can solve many problems with these resources. It's not necessary to fight, because the enemy will disappear when we become Earth Nation.

For example, your right arm doesn't hurt or beat up your left foot. If you do that, you will suffer because it is your own body. So here is the point, it would be so ridiculous for Fukushima prefecture to attack Okayama prefecture.

Alright then what are we going to spend that huge defense budget on?
Use it to protect the Earth Nation!! From what?

Use it for protection against Deforestation, Drought, Ozone Layer Depletion, Global Warming, and Natural disasters (such as Typhoons, Earthquakes, Tsunamis, Environmental destruction 〈Most environmental destruction is caused by man isn't it?〉). Restore the rainforest.

もう１つ大切な事は、エイズやガンなどの病気から私達人間を守る。私達は今現在の生活から大昔の生活に戻る事は出来ません。それでは今現在の生活を保てるように、破壊してしまった森林を作れば良いのです。

　もっとソーラー（天からの恵み太陽熱＝タダ）や風力を普及させれば良いのです。
　オゾン層のための研究や地震予知や地球温暖化をくい止める為の研究や、起こってしまった竜巻や台風を海上に誘導出来ないかの研究や、エイズやガンの治療薬の研究や普及に防衛費を使うべきです。

　戦争のために戦闘機を作るのではなく、宇宙ステーションを作り、維持するためや、より高度な天気予報の研究や、通信やGPS等のために人工衛星を打ち上げる

　アフリカでたくさんの人々が病気で苦しんでいます。地球国は１つです。体のどこかが調子が悪いとその人の体全体は健康を保てません。自分勝手に狭い視野で物事を考え、「自分の回りさえ良ければいい」と言っても、地球国のどこかの地域が不健康ではバランスを保てません。

Another important thing is to protect humans from diseases such as AIDS and cancer etc. We cannot return to the ancient way of living. To keep today's lifestyle, we should rebuild and heal the damaged rainforest.

We must spread more solar energy and wind power　(free blessing from heaven).

We should spend more money for research study of the ozone layer. Create systems to predict earthquakes, develop better devices to redirect tornadoes and typhoons that occur on land out to sea. Research remedy for AIDS and cancer.

Launch satellites to build and maintain the space stations for study and research that will enhance the advanced weather forecasts. For communications, and GPS, etc. Rather than building weapons.

Many people in Africa suffer from illnesses. The Earth Nation is one. If something is wrong with any part of your body, the body as a hole cannot maintain good health. You can't be selfish, look or think only from your point of view. If you say "I'm ok with happiness only around me." We cannot maintain balance if there are unhealthy regions anywhere in the world.

地球上が一国になれば、地球上全体を住みやすい状態にする必要があります。これは難しい事ではありません。なぜなら現在の個々のどの国々もプラスマイナス０、どの国も損も得もしないけれど、地球上の全人類と全生物にとっては得とプラスになるからです。

　では、もし地球国が出来たとしましょう。外枠は素晴らしいものが出来ました。コンピューターでいうとハードの部分です。でも中身（そこに生きる私達人類）すなわちソフトの部分が変わらなければ日々の事件や事故、犯罪や暴力やいじめや差別などは無くならないでしょう。

　しかし、それにも解決の答えがあるのです。いくつかのキーワードがあるので１つ１つ説明していきましょう。

① 　真実を知る＝強さ＝正しい生き方
② 　人間の弱さ＝愚かさ＝間違いを認め＝許し、正す

③ 　どう生きる＝どう考える＝どう行動する
④ 　宗教に違いはない＝win・win シチュエーション
⑤ 　目に見えないもの＝最も大切、尊い

If the earth becomes one nation, it is necessary to make the whole earth live in good conditions. It is not difficult. Because every individual country is plus minus zero, neither country is no gain, but it is a big profit for all humanity and all living things on earth.

Now, let's say that an Earth Nation has been created. The outer frame is wonderful. Like the hard part of a computer, Well then, if the contents (which is human beings living there), is soft parts of computer, if we do not change, daily incidents, accidents, crimes, violence, bullying and discrimination will not disappear.

But that also has a solution. There are several keywords, so let's explain them one by one.

① Know the truth = Strength = Correct way of life
② Human　weakness = Stupidity = Acknowledge mistakes = Forgive and correct
③ How to live = How to think = How to act
④ There is no difference in religion = win・win situation
⑤ Invisible = Most important and precious

２、真実を知る

①真実を知る＝正しい情報を得るという事は、正しく判断し決断し、正しく生きるためには必要不可欠です。

　たとえば最近、栄養ドリンクやサプリメントが注目されていますが、それを例に取りますと、その商品の中に入っている、含まれている栄養素は正しく表示されていますが、その栄養素がすべて体の中に吸収される訳ではないのです。

　例えば、体がカルシウムを吸収するためには、カルシウムの半分の量のマグネシウムが必要です。ですからカルシウムが単品で入っているものをいくら採っても体には吸収されることなくそのカルシウムは、ただ体を素通りして出てしまいます。

　レモン何個分のビタミンＣと言っても、確かにその商品にはそれだけの量は入っていますが、それがすべて体に吸収されている訳ではないのです。とすると相乗効果や日本では昔から食い合わせなどと言っていますが、その知識を知る必要がある訳です。

　北朝鮮では国民に必要な情報や真実を伝えず国民のマインド をコントロールしています。これに近い事は他の国々でも大なり小なりあるのでは？

2、 *Know the truth*

① Knowing the truth = Obtaining the correct information
is necessary for making correct decisions and living correctly.
It is absolutely necessary.

For example, recently nutritional drinks and supplements have been getting attention. The nutrients contained in the product are correctly displayed, but all of the nutrients displayed are not absorbed in the body.

The body needs half the amount of magnesium to absorb calcium, therefore no matter how much calcium is taken as a single item it will not be absorbed by the body. The calcium will simply pass through the body and exit.

Even if you say how many lemons of vitamin C, that a product contains, all of it. You should know the synergistic effects. Japanese people have said KUIAWSE.
(KUIAWASE ; To eat foods thought to upset the stomach if eaten in combination)

North Korea control the mind of the people by not giving necessary information or truth. Isn't there something similar big or small in other countries?

奴隷の時代『黒人は白人よりも劣っている、だから奴隷制度は正しい』と思い込んでいた人間が大勢いました。

　このような間違った情報や知らされていなかった真実などを知れば過去の過ちから学習し、正しく考え、正しく生きる事が出来るのです。

Not so long ago, there were many people who believed that "black people more inferior to white people, and that slavery was right".

Knowing such wrong information and the unknown truth. We can learn from past mistakes. Then we can think right and live correctly.

３、人間の弱さ

②人間は誰しも完璧ではない、だから人間なのですが。人間は権力欲、支配欲、妬み、恨みといった悪魔が支配する感情や気持ちも持ち合わせています。

　しかし、それらの感情は破滅こそ招くものの、愛、平和、幸せを生み出す事には繋がって行きません。

　ですが、人間が自分自身の弱さも愚かさも知れば、そこから出た結果を認識し、間違いならそれを認め、正す事が出来ます。そうする事で本来人間があるべき姿や、生き方が出来るのです。

　南アフリカでネルソン・マンデラ元大統領がアパルトヘイトで過ちを犯した人々への仕返し（復讐）Revengeを止めるために、白人の人達に自分の過ち、罪を認め、公にオープンにし、反省した者は許す、罪を課さないという法律を考えました。すばらしい事です！
許すというのは慈愛（神の愛）です。

　ここで最も重要な事は先ず自分を許すという事です。なぜなら、自分を許せない人は他人も許せないからです。という事は自分を許せる人は他人も許せるのです。

3、 *Human weakness*

② Humans are not perfect, that's why we are humans.
 Some humans have bad demonic spirits of domination from the devil, such as power lust, desire of control, jealousy, and grudges.
 These feelings lead to ruin, they do not create or produce love, peace, or happiness.

 But if humans know their weaknesses and stupidity, they can recognize the consequences. If they are wrong, they should acknowledge and correct them. By doing so, we can create what humans should be and how to live.

 The former president of South Africa Nelson Mandelae ask the oppressors of apartheid to confess they're crimes against humanity own up to it. He spoke against violent revenge. Forgiveness is a great charity of affection "The love of God"

 The most important thing here is to forgive yourself first. The reason is one who cannot forgive yourself, you cannot forgive others. This means that someone who can forgive oneself can forgive others.

４、どう生きる

③人生をより良く生きるための基本は感謝です 人間は humble（謙虚）な attitude（態度、姿勢）を持つべきです。なぜならそれらからは争い、戦い、妬み、憎しみが生まれないからです。

今の自分の現状に不満を持っている人はいますか？

この問いかけに多くの人々の答えは Yes でしょう。

その中で前向きな不満、今よりももっと良くなるぞ！今日の自分より明日の自分は向上しているぞ！！ という意味の現状に満足していない＝不満は前向きで良いのですが、なんで自分はこんな状況に置かれているんだ、こんなはずではない、といった不満は自分自身の考え方や態度を変える事で状況も変わります。

昔、子供向けのアニメで『良かった！』を探すという女の子（ポリアンナ）が出て来る物語を、私の娘がまだ小さい時に一緒に観た事があります。まさにこれは人生の基本を子供達にわかりやすく教 えていると思いました。

たくさんの大人の人達にもぜひ観て頂きたいアニメです。『良かったを探す』＝『良かった、ありがとう』と感謝しているのです。

4、 *How to live*

③ The basis for living a better life is appreciation/gratitude. Humans should have a humble attitude. Because humility does not create fights, battles, envy, or hatred.

If you ask anyone if they are dissatisfied with their present situation.

Most people will answer Yes! to this question.

Among them, positive dissatisfaction, it will be better than it is now! Tomorrow will be better than today!! I am not satisfied with the current situation = dissatisfaction is good, but who has dissatisfaction like [Why am I in this situation, this shouldn't be.] People who have these kinds of complaints, you can change the situation by changing one's way of thinking and attitude.

Years ago, when my daughter was a kid, we were watching a good animation for children called "Pollyanna". The character Pollyanna always found good in everything. I thought this was a very easy way to teach children the basics of life.

This is an animation that many adults should watch too. [Searched for good things] = [Thank goodness] It shows appreciation.

どんな厳しい状況に置かれていても感謝出来る事は必ずあります。仕事もなくスラム街で日々暴力や怒りの中で生活している人々でも、たとえば朝目覚めたら『今日も目覚めさせて下さってありがとうございます』と感謝する事が出来ます

　食事をする時、いくら質素な物でも『食糧を与えて下さってありがとうございます』　寝る前に『今日一日ありがとうございました』と感謝する事が出来ます。常に自分は神様の大きな慈愛に包まれて生きている事を知るべきです。神様の慈愛が分からない人は母の愛を想像して下さい。母は自分の子供に 対して大きな愛を持っています（シャーリー・シーザーの NO CHARGE は母の愛を歌った唄です）。

　「徳を積む」 事がその人の魂を向上させる事に繋がるのですが、徳を積むためには愛を与える事（自分にも他人にも）が最も重要な事です。

　愛にもいろいろありますが、「受け入れる愛」「許す愛」「信じる愛」。受け入れる愛とは無条件に人や自分を受け入れる、認めるという事です。
　許す愛とは人や自分の犯してしまった過ちを許すという事。信じる愛とは人や自分を信じる事。どれもむずかしい事です。
　ですが、どれも愛です。

No matter how difficult the situation is, there's always gratitude. Even people who live in violence and anger in slums every day without work, can still appreciate waking up in the morning and saying, "Thank you God for waking me up and giving me another day."

When you eat, no matter how simple that meal is, "Thank you for giving me food." Before you go to bed, you can be grateful, "Thank you for today." You should always know that you are living under the great affection of God. If you do not understand God's charity love, please imagine your mother's love. A mother has a great love for her children (Shirley Caesar's NO CHARGE is a song of mother's love)

"Build virtue" leads to improving one's soul, Giving love(both to yourself and others)is the most important thing to build virtue.

There are various kinds of love, "Accept love" "Forgive love" " Believe love " . Accepting love means the unconditional compliance and approval of a person or yourself.
Forgive love means forgive the mistakes that others and yourself have made. Believing love means believing in a person or yourself.
It's all difficult, but all is love.

そして神様は 今まで私たち人間にたくさんの愛を下さっています。真実を知り、正しい行い、良い行いをすると気持ちの良いものです。他人を思いやる、他人を助ける、人から見返りを期待しないでする行いが真の行いです。人からの見返りよりも神様からの見返り（ご褒美）を期待して下さい。

　人間とは小さなものです。
　問題の解決策も、ご褒美も神様が与えて下さるものは私達人間が想像もつかない素晴らしい、ちっぽけな私達人間の頭では考えもおよばないような方法だったり、物だったり、事だったりするのです。

　ギブアップとはあきらめるという意味ではなく、両手を上げ、天にかかげ、Give・it・up 自分は一生懸命やった！
　出来る限りの事は尽くした！
　あとは天の神様にまかせるという意味に使うべきでしょう。

And God has given unlimited love to humans. It feels good to know the truth, do the right things, and do good things. Consideration of others, helping others. True act is what you do without expecting a reward from someone. Please expect the reward from God rather than the reward from man.

Humans are small things.

The solution of the problem and the reward are the things that God gives us, which we humans cannot imagine, It's a method, thing, or thing that we humans can't think of.

Give up doesn't mean giving up, but raising both hands, holding them to the sky, Give・it・up I did my best!

I've done everything I can!
Leave the rest to God in heaven(Let go and let God).

5、宗教に違いはない

④　神様（God）の存在を否定する人がいますが、その人たちは神様（God）の存在に気付き感謝する素晴らしい経験をまだしていないからでしょう。

　あなたも神の子です。

　あなたがシャッターを閉じ、　目と耳を閉ざしている間は、神様はあなたのことは見守ってくれていますがそれだけです。

　あなたから神様に話しかけて、はじめて神様もあなたに答えてくれるのです。なぜなら神様はそれほど尊い存在（Most high）だからです。

　地球上には数々の宗教があります。

　神を崇める、誉め讃える、感謝することは素晴らしいことです。

　その素晴らしいことをしている人々がなぜその宗教のことで争うのでしょうか？

　この争いも真実を知って神様の言葉に従えば無くなります。答えは簡単です。

　あなたが信じている神も教えも、隣の人が信じている神も教えも、同じ神、神は１つですという事です。（神様は人間 ではないので一人とは言わない）

5、 *There is no difference in religion*

④ There are people who deny the existence of God, because they are aware of the existence of God and haven't had such a wonderful experience of thank God yet.

You are also a child of God.

God is just watching over you as long as you close the shutter and close your eyes and ears.

Only when you speak to God, God will answer you. Because God is such a precious existence(Most high).

There are many religions on earth.

It is a wonderful thing to worship, praise, and thank God.

But why do the people doing that wonderful thing have disputes about the religion?

This dispute will disappear if you know the truth and follow the word of God. The answer is simple.

The God and the teaching you believe in, and the God and teaching the neighbor believes in, is the same God, God is one. (God is not a human, so you don't call alone)

この世の光と闇、宇宙、太陽、地球、すべての創造主、愛の源、それが神です。
　ただその神のことを人々が違う呼び名で呼んでいるだけなのです（広い地球上言葉が違うのと同じです）それによってちがう宗教と枠をこれまた、人間が作って決めつけているのです。

　信仰とは（私は信と行と書きたい）そうすると字のごとく、信じる事を行う。
　これこそが神と通じる手段なのです。
　人々が神のことをゴッドと呼ぼうがアッラーと呼ぼうがジェホバと呼ぼうがヤハウェと呼ぼうがラスタファリと呼ぼうがロードと呼ぼうが神様と呼ぼうが、呼び名は言語と同じで違っても良いのです。
　ただその神に感謝し、祈る気持ちが奇跡を起こさせるのです。

　そして仏教も、*もともとは神の教えや言葉を世界中に伝えるために Jesus の弟子達が回って説いた教えが長い年月をかけて人から人へと伝わっていく際に、少しずつ源は神の教えなのにそれを伝えた人々（人間）へと対象が変わっていった のでしょう。
*私的思想

The light and darkness of the world, the universe, the sun, the Earth, all the creators, the source of love, that is God.

It's just that people call it differently (just like the different words on the broad globe). Human being make and set different religions and frame their own decisions.

Faith (I want to write belief and action) Then, like a letter, we do what we believe.

This is the way to communicate with God.

It doesn't matter if you call God, Allah, Jehovah, Yahweh, Rastafari, Lord, or Kamisama, is the same as the language.

It's okay to call different names.

Just thankful to God and praying causes miracles.

About Buddhism (*) Originally, Jesus' disciples went around to preach to teach God's teaching and words to the world.

When passing on from person to person over the years, the object of worship has changed to the people(human) who told it, even though it was originally the teaching of God.

*(Personal thought/ideology)

私的思想ついでにもう一つ、私が皆様と共有したい考えに『自殺はなぜしてはいけないか』をお伝えしたいと思います。神様は非常に慈悲深いとは先程も申し上げました、人は完璧ではなく愚かで弱い生き物ですので、失敗や過ちも犯します。

　が、自分が気付き改心し神に赦しを請うと神は許して下さいます。ただその方法や内容は本人と神との間の事です。

　では自殺をした人は神のルールの中で最も重い罪（神が与えて下さった命を自ら絶つ）を犯す訳ですが、自殺をするという事は貴方の周りの多くの人々（家族、友人、知人＝神の子）をも、悲しめ苦しめる訳ですから罪は尚更重いです。神から頂いた命を絶ってしまって は、冒頭の Judgement day の場には行けず神に赦しを請う事が出来ないという事です。すなわち地獄行きが確定で避けられないという事です。

　地獄とは貴方がつらく逃れたかった苦しみの何十倍もの苦しみが肉体的にも精神的にもずーっと続く場所です。

　逃れるつもりが現状よりも酷い場所に行くとは本末転倒です。自殺をしたい人が今現在逃れたいと苦しんでいる状況はその人には超えられるものです。

　自分と神を信じて下さい。現状は改善されて行きます！ 貴方が想像もしなかった方法で。

One more personal thought/ideology I would like to share with you which is [Why you shouldn't suicide] I said earlier that God is very merciful. Human beings are foolish and weak creatures. We are not perfect! That's why we make mistakes and fail.

But if you realize that you are converted and ask forgiveness to God, God will forgive you. However, the forgiveness method and contents are between you and God.

So the person who commits suicide has made the heaviest sin in God's rule (Cut off the life that God has given) Sin is even more serious, because committing suicide also causes many people around you (family, friends, acquaintances = child of God) to grieve and suffer. If you lose the life that God has given you, you can't go to the place of Judgment Day and ask God for forgiveness. In other words, going to hell is fixed and unavoidable.

Hell is a place where dozens of times the suffering that you have wanted to escape has continued, both ways physically and mentally.

You are going to a place much worse than you are now. That's getting one's priorities wrong/putting the cart before the horse. The situation you want to escape you can be surpass /overcome.

Believe in yourself and God. The current situation is improving! In a way you never imagined.

6、目に見えないもの

⑤　私たちが生きているこの世の中には目に見える物、手で触れられる物・物体と、そうではない目には見えない物とが存在します。たとえば、愛、魂（ソウル）、命、心、精神（スピリット）、気持ち、考え（アイデア）、勇気、平和、空気、教育、マナー、記憶、思い出、態度、音楽、言葉、これら目に見えない物こそ、昔から人間が生きて来た中で最も大切な物、事です。

　目に見える物、物質はお金で買えます。何かのコマーシャルでプライスレス（お金で買えない物）に価値があるというようなメッセージのものがありましたが、その通りだと思います。そしてこの目に見えない物をたくさん持っている 人、目に見えない物が充実している人が真の Rich man（富豪者）なのです。

　そして、これらは人間誰もが平等に得るチャンスがあるものです。ただその存在を知り、欲すれば良いのです。
　しかし、その存在を 知らなければ欲しようとは思わない、そこに問題があるのです。
　しかし、その問題は解決出来ます。
　地球上の人間1人1人にこの存在を知らせれば良いのです。そして感謝すれば良いのです。
　空気の存在に感謝した事がある方がどの位おられるでしょうか？
　アストロノット（宇宙飛行士）は YES かも。

6、 *Invisible*

⑤ In this world where we live, there are things that are visible, things that you can touched by hands, and things that are not visible. For example, love, soul, life, heart, spirit, feeling, thought(idea), courage, peace, air, education, manners, remembrance, memories, attitudes, music, words, The things that cannot be seen are the most important things since ancient times.

You can buy visible things /substances with money. There were some commercials with a message saying (things that can't be bought with money) are priceless and valuable. I think this is true. And those who have a lot of invisible things are the true rich human.

The opportunities for everyone to be equal is to know its existence and want it.

If you don't know its existence, you won't want it. That's a problem!

But that problem can be solved.

All we have to do is to inform each human being on the earth of this existence. And be thankful.

How many people have been grateful for the existence of air?

Maybe astronauts are YES.

神の目から見れば誰もが幸せに生きる権利を平等に持っています。しかし実際私たちが生きている今日、被害者があまりにも多くいます。これは人災です。

　この世に生を受けたという事は母体、母親から生まれてきた訳です。でも中にはこの目に見えない最も大切な物や事を与える・伝える母親や家族に恵まれていない人がいます。
　なぜならその親も家族も本当に必要なもの、大切なものというのを知らないから、与え伝えようとしないのです。もしくは間違って、変えて伝えている、（Jesus の容姿の時のように）。これは悪循環　（Bad サークル）です。目に見えないものは自分が経験したり、持っていたりしなければ伝える事は難しいし、その子供は知らずに育ちます。

　たとえば一番簡単な例をあげますと、ある日 私が電車に乗って席に座っていました。そこにおばあちゃまとお孫さんが乗って来たので私はおばあちゃまに席を譲るために立ち上がり『どうぞおかけ下さい』と声をかけました。
　するとどうでしょう！
　このおばあちゃまは『あら、どうもありがとう』と言って自分は座らないで孫を座らせたのです。

From the eyes of God, everyone has equally the privilege to live happily. But in fact, as we are living today, there are too many victims. This is a man-made disaster.

Being born into this world means born from a mother/mother's body. However, there are some who are not blessed with mothers and families who are supposed to give and convey these invisible and most important things.

If neither of the parents nor the family know what is really necessary and important, they will not give and pass it on. Or, teaching the wrong way as in Jesus' appearance. This is a vicious circle (Bad circle). It is difficult to convey invisible things unless you experience it or have it yourself, if not a child grows up unknowingly.

For example, a very simple case. One day I was sitting on a train. A grandmother and her grandson get on the train, so I stood up to give up my seat and said, "Please sit here"

How would it be!
"Oh, thank you very much". Said the grandma, but instead of sitting herself, she let her grandson sit down.

ここでおばあちゃまは大変な間違いを犯しました。

　小さな孫が電車がゆれて転ぶと危ないと思ったのでしょうが、それならば自分が座って自分の膝に孫を座らせるべきだったのです。そしてこの孫が目の前で「他人が目上の人に席を譲る場面をライブで経験する、目にするチャンス」をも奪ったのです。

　疲れている私は自分よりも若い、しかもエネルギーが有り余っている子供に席を譲るくらいなら私が座っていたかったです。

　そして、こうして育った孫達が今の若者達で、社会は『最近の若者はお年寄りに席も譲らない！』と言いますが、この孫達は『席は自分が座るものだ』と身を持って学習して来た訳ですから、また誰かが『席はお年寄りや体の不自由な人に譲るもの』と再教育するか、自分で経験しなければこの若者の身には付きません。

　なぜなら、これ（席を譲る）をマスターする、自然に行えるようになるには少々時間がかかるからです。まず、① 真実を知る。席はお年寄りや体の不自由な人たちに譲るんだという事を知る。

　知ったら実際電車に乗ってそのチャンスが来た時、きっと最初は『どうぞ、おかけ下さい』と言って席を立つ事が出来ないと思います。

　なぜならそれには、⑤ 勇気が必要だからです。

Here Granny made a terrible mistake.

Perhaps she thought her grandson would fall when the train sways. If so she should have sat down and sat her grandson on her lap. Granny also missed the opportunity to teach her grandson courtesy to others in real time.

I was very tired, I would have liked to keep my seat rather than give it up to a young child who's more energetic than I.
Grandchildren who grew up in this way are now young people of today.

Society says, "Recently young passengers don't give up their seats to the elderly". There is a need to re-educate and teach that giving your seat to the elderly and the disabled is common courtesy. If you do not experience it yourself, it will be difficult to acquire the young generation.

Because it takes some time to master this (giving up your seat) and be able to do it naturally. First, ① You must know the truth. The seat should be given to the elderly and people with disabilities.

When you know this, you will be able to get on the train when the opportunity arise to do the right thing. I don't think the first time you can say and do, 'Please have a seat,' and stand up then give it up your seat.

Because it takes ⑤ Need courage!

私も今はなんの躊躇もなく自然に出来ますが、若い頃、良い事なのにそれをするための最初の一言『どうぞ』がなかなか口から出ず、お年寄りと目が合うのを待ったり、もし『次の駅で降りますから』と断られたら恥ずかしいなどといろんな事を考え、とうとう言えずじまいという経験を何度もしたことがあります。勇気なんですね、これも。

　ここで、目に見えないものいわゆる勇気も必要になってきます。

　②大人達が間違いに気付き、正し、それを変えていく努力をしなければなりませんが、『小さな事からコツコツと』誰かの言葉じゃないですが、日々の生活の中で自分にも出来るのです、若者が席を譲ってくれたら断らずに次の駅で降りるとしても『ありがとう』と言ってとりあえず座ってあげる。

　これも昔近所の大人みんなで子供達を育てた•教えたのと同じ事を社会が意識して行えば良いのです。

　なぜなら、現在は近所が最初の章でも言いましたがズームアップされて広くなっているのです。

　このように親や家族に正しく与えてもらえずに、もしくはその親や家族が居なく育った人達も、社会で•地球規模で　①真実を知らせ、②間違いを認め正し、⑤目に見えないものの大切さを教え、③　どう生きるか導いてあげる事は出来ます。

I can do it naturally now without hesitation, but when I was young, the first word of "please" didn't come out of my mouth. Even though it's a good thing, I waited for eye contact with the elderly person, also if the person said "I'll get off at the next station, No thank you", such a declined might have been embarrassing.

This thing needed in order to take action, such as common courtesy, consideration courage.

②Adults must be aware of mistakes correct them, and make efforts to change them. Like someone's words "Steadily do it from small things". You can do it yourself in your daily life. For example, if young people give up their seats, even if you get off at the next station, without refusing, you say "Thank you" and sit down for the time being.

A long time ago all the adults in the neighborhood raised and taught children, society should be aware of the same thing now.

Because now the neighborhood is zoomed up and wider, as I said in the first chapter. Growing up without giving correctness from parents and family.

Even those who grew up without parents or family, We can in society • Globally ① Tell the truth, ② Admit mistakes and correct them, ⑤ Teach the importance of invisible things, ③Guide how to live.

人間が本当に幸せに生きるという事は自分次第で出来ます。
　これをきっかけに自分と地球上すべての生き物が平和で愛に満ちあふれた生き方が出来る事を祈り努力して行きましょう。

It's up to you to live happily. I hope this will be a catalyst.

Let's pray through all of our endeavors that all living things on earth can live in peace and exist altogether in a loving way of life.

おわりに

　最後にこの本の最初に述べた地球国の事についてもう少し触れておきます。

　私達が住んでいるこの地球が出来てから相当な年月が経っています。

　それは過去にこの地球上に存在した生物たち（人間も含めて）が、地球を痛めつけず地球からの恩恵を感謝して受け、自然の循環にその役割の一員として生活して来たからでしょう。

　たとえばあなたの家なりアパート全体なりが、壁は剥がれ落ち、雨はもる、床は抜ける、トイレは詰まる、建物全体が傾くなどという事になり、修復不可能になった場合、

　あなたならどうしますか？
　よそへ引っ越すか取り壊して立て直しますよね？

　しかし、私達地球上に住む生命体は地球以外に引っ越す事は、今現在は無理です。
　地球を壊したら創り直す事は私達人間には無理です。

　となると自分達が生きている今は まだなんとか住めるが、子孫達は住める状態ではなくなってくるのでは？

Epilogue

Finally, I would like to tell you a little more about the "Earth Nation" I mention at the beginning of this book.

Quite a long time have passed since the creation of this planet, which we live on "The Earth"

That's because the life that existed on this planet in the past (including humans) did not harm the Earth and gratefully received benefit and lived their lives as part of the natural circulation. But humans are living so arrogantly today that they pollute, damage, and change the ecosystem of the planet.

For example, your house or your entire apartment is irreparable damage like the walls are peeling off, it rains, the floor comes off, the toilet is clogged, the entire building is tilted, etc.

What are you going to do?

You move to another place or demolish it and rebuild it, right?

But we, life forms that live on the earth, right now we can't move to another planet other than the earth.

If we destroy our planet, it is impossible for us humans to recreate earth.

In that case, we can still manage to live for now, but our descendants may not be able to live.

住めるというよりは生きていくのが困難な状況になるでしょう。ですので、今から未来のために私たち人間が犯してしまった過ちをくり返さず、修復出来る事は早急にする必要があります。

　なぜなら信用と同じで、失うのは一瞬ですが、取り戻すのには長い年月と努力が必要だからです。

　地球国になれば、自然面でもビジネスの面でも今以上に潤い活性化するはずです。自然の面から言うと今現在のように貧困地区と先進地区のように偏りがなく地球全体の底上げが出来ます。

　たとえば干ばつで食糧がなく人々が餓死しているような地域から人間は、よそへ移り住みそこには太陽熱（エネルギー）を、作り、送る巨大プロジェクトを建設します。海底や地下にケーブルをひき、地球上で人間が住む地域と、野生動物が生息する地域、工業地域、生産地域などと大きく地域を作るのです。

　あと、ビジネス面では地球上で自由参入出来るのですから技術やアイデアなどを持っている会社は世界中どこででもビジネスが出来る訳です。

It will be difficult to even exist. We will not repeat the mistakes we humans have made. If we are to have a future on earth it is necessary and urgent to repair it now.

Because, like credit, you lose it for a moment, but it takes years and effort to get it back.

When we become "Earth Nation" nature and business both terms will be more activated. From a natural point of view, it is possible to raise the level of the whole world without being biased to poor areas and the advanced area as it is now.

For example, humans move away from areas where people are starving to death due to drought and lack of food. We must build a huge project there, to create and send solar heat (energy). By pulling cables on the seabed and underground, improving large areas such as where humans live, where wild animals live, industrial areas, production areas, etc.

Also, in terms of business, companies that have technologies and ideas can do business anywhere in the world because they can freely enter the world.

今現在都道府県間で行なっている事を現在の国同士で行うだけの事ですので、お互いに尊重し合い win-win シュチュエーションで事を行えば、今よりいろんなハードルがとっぱらわれるのですから、より良い方向に向かいますよね。

　各国間の違いや変化も互いのルールを尊重すれば問題ないです。例えば京都ではある一定の地域では高層ビルの建設は NG ですし、いろんな観光地でもよく有るコンビニの外観もその地域にマッチした物にしていますよね？

　その地域（元は国）ではその地域に合わせて尊重して生活もビジネスも行えば何の問題もないです。

What we are currently doing between prefectures is just what we are going to do between current countries. Respect each other and do things in a win-win situation and various hurdles will be removed, so we will move in a better direction.

There is no problem with differences and changes between countries as long as they respect each other's rules. For example, in Kyoto, construction of skyscrapers is NG in certain areas. The appearance of convenience stores in various tourist spots also matches the area, right?

In that area　(formerly a country), there is no problem if you live and do business with respect for that area.

ここまで読んで下さった方々へ、地球国の事はまだまだ沢山アイデアやビジョンがありますし、精神的な思考のお話も、皆様に直接お話させて頂く機会（講演）などでディスカッションが出来れば幸いです。

　終わりにこの本を書く事を私に与えて下さった神様に感謝します。
　そして、その事をサポートしてくれた夫、子供達に感謝します。私の人生のファンデーションを創ってくれた母 阿津子、父 孝 、日本とアメリカの家族達 Love ya！

　今まで出会った人々と、これから出会うであろう人々に感謝します。
　神様の願いを理解して下さる方々へ『お会い出来る事を楽しみにしています』

　愛してます。ついてる。嬉しい。楽しい。感謝します。幸福です。有難うございます。許します。
　愛は無償
　神からあなたへのメッセージ
　内から外へ／外見は内面を表し
　自分自身を愛すべし

アンティー ヤカ

To those who have read till here, I'm so happy and there are still many ideas and visions about the "Earth Nation". We can also discuss spiritual thoughts at the opportunity (lecture) to talk directly to everyone.

Finally, I thank God for giving me the vision for this book.

Thank you to my husband and children who supported me. Mother Atsuko and Father Takashi who created the foundation of my life. Japanese and American families Love ya！

I thank the people I have met already, and the people I will meet in the future.

To those who understand God's wishes, "I'm looking forward to seeing you."

Love. Blessing. Joy. Fun. Appreciate. Happy. Thank you. Forgive.

Love Is No Charge

Message 2 U from GOD

Inside Out

U Gotta Love Yourself (UGLY)

2gether 2strong

By Auntie Yaka

【著者プロフィール】
　アメリカ人のソウルシンガーの妻、3 人の子供たちの母、
芸能音楽事務所の経営者。社名 LINC は Love Is No Charge
（愛は無償）の頭文字。

　岡山県生まれ。6 歳から大阪で育ち、21 歳で上京。23 歳
で結婚出産、28 年間埼玉県に住み、現在は東京在住。

【問い合わせ先】
株式会社 LINC
　〒150-0031　東京都渋谷区桜丘町 23 番 17 号
　　　　　　　　シティコート桜丘 408
　　　　佐藤　八代子
　E-mail：linc.inc3782 @gmail.com

地球国創世（キリストは黒人）
2021 年 5 月 5 日 第 1 刷発行
　著　者　Auntie Yaka
　翻　訳　Yayoko N Satoh
　発行者　釣部 人裕
　発行所　万代宝書房
　〒176-0002 東京都練馬区桜台 1-6-9-102
　　　　電話 080-3916-9383　FAX 03-6914-5474
　　　　ホームページ：http://bandaiho.com/
　　　　メール：info@bandaiho.com
　印刷・製本　小野高速印刷株式会社
　落丁本・乱丁本は小社でお取替え致します。
　　© Auntie Yaka 2021 Printed in Japan
　ISBN　978-4- 910064-37-6　C0036

装丁・デザイン 小林由香

【Profile】

The wife of an American soul singer, the mother of three children, and the owner of an entertainment agency. The company's name LINC is an acronym for Love Is No Charge.

Born in Okayama prefecture, grew up in Osaka from the age of 6, and moved to Tokyo at the age of 21. Married and gave birth at the age of 23, lived in Saitama prefecture for 28 years, and now lives in Tokyo.

【Contact】
LINC inc.
 #408 Citycourt Sakuragaoka23-17
 Sakuragaoka-cho, Shibuya-ku,Tokyo, 150-0031
       Yayoko Satoh
 E-mail：linc.inc3782 @gmail.com

The Earth Nation Creation 〔Jesus Is A Brother〕

5th, May,2021 First print issuance
  Author   Auntie Yaka
  Translator Yayoko N Satoh
  Issuer   Hitohiro Tsuribe
  Publisher Bandaiho Shobo
   1-6-9-102 Sakuradai Nerima-ku Tokyo 〒176-0002
        TEL   080-3916-9383   FAX 03-6914-5474
        Home page：http://bandaiho.com/
        E-mail：info@bandaiho.com
    Printing/Binding   Ono Kousoku Insatsu Co,Ltd

  We will replace the missing or incorrect pages.
    © Auntie Yaka 2021 Printed in Japan
    ISBN   978-4-910064-37-6   C0036

  Binding・Design   Yuka Kobayashi

万代宝書房について

　みなさんのお仕事・志など、未常識だけど世の中にとって良いもの（こと）はたくさんあります。社会に広く知られるべきことはたくさんあります。社会に残さなくてはいけない思い・実績があります！　それを出版という形で国会図書館に残します！

「万代宝書房」は、「『人生は宝』、その宝を『人類の宝』まで高め、歴史に残しませんか？」をキャッチにジャーナリスト釣部人裕が二〇一九年七月に設立した出版社です。

「実語教」（平安時代末期から明治初期にかけて普及していた庶民のための教訓を中心とした初等教科書。江戸時代には寺子屋で使われていたそうです）という千年もの間、読み継がれた道徳の教科書に『富は一生の宝、知恵は万代の宝』という節があり、「お金はその人の一生を豊かにするだけだが、知恵は何世代にも引き継がれ多くの人の共通の宝となる」いう意味からいただきました。

誕生間がない若い出版社ですので、アマゾンと自社サイトでの販売を基本としています。多くの読者と著者の共感をと支援を心よりお願いいたします。

　２０１９年７月８日

　　　　　　　　　　　　　　万代宝書房